PROMPT RESPONSE

Prompt Response

Ruth Y. Nott

Chiefland, FL, USA

PROMPT RESPONSE

To obtain autographed copies of this book or obtain required permission for use of material herein, email author at: ruth@ruthnott.com

www.ruthnott.com

ISBN-13:
978-1494974039

ISBN-10:
1494974037

Printed in the United States of America
by Create Space Independent Publishing Platform

Other Titles By This Author

A Pure and Simple Faith

Crazy Patch

Where Memory Lingers

Haiku for Lovers

Garden of Faith

Family Matters

Family Matters, Vol. II

After the Rain

Here on My Knees

All There Is

Preface

Webster's New World Dictionary © 2003

poem – an arrangement of words, esp. a rhythmical composition, sometimes rhymed, in a style more imaginative than ordinary speech or prose

Dictionary.com © 2014

po·em - ***noun***

1. – a composition in verse, especially one that is characterized by a highly developed artistic form and by the use of heightened language and rhythm to express an intensely imaginative interpretation of the subject.
2. – composition that, though not in verse, is characterized by great beauty of language or expression: a prose poem from the Scriptures; a symphonic poem.
3. – something having qualities that are suggestive of or likened to those of poetry: *Marcel, that chicken cacciatore was an absolute poem.*

prose **[prohz]** - *Noun*

1. – the ordinary form of spoken or written language, without metrical structure, as distinguished from poetry or verse.
2. – matter-of-fact, commonplace, or dull expression, quality, discourse, etc.

PROMPT RESPONSE

Definitions are arbitrary and open to interpretation. What one person calls poetry may be prose or ordinary writing to another.

I lay no claim to expertise in poetry. What I write comes from the heart or a lively imagination, written quickly or with lengthy thought and intense examination. It just comes. It is what it is.

****

As the title of this book indicates, most of what I have written during the past year has been in response to weekly or daily poetry prompts provided by the good folks and readers of Robert Lee Brewer's Poetic Asides Blog on the web at www.writersdigest.com.

I present them here as the year progressed, showing the date and the prompt; however, very few were written on the date of the prompt, some being written months later when the mood struck me to sit down and write again. Those poems which have no prompt indicated are unprompted except by a nudge from my muse. As I age, time speeds by and thoughts slow to a crawl. Bear with me and I hope you enjoy the poems of 2013.

Ruth Y. Nott

PROMPT RESPONSE

This book is dedicated to Sasha and Bucky, (Papillon mix and Boston Terrier shown in the cover photo) my precious fur-babies who keep me company, keep me entertained and show me daily that I am loved.

PROMPT RESPONSE

PROMPT RESPONSE

2013

1-2-13 – Prompt - The poem can list New Year resolutions, show a person resolved to do something, or any other unique angle you resolve to write.

January first
Each year new resolutions
Too soon broken

1-2-13 – Prompt - Write a poem about parenting, becoming a parent, or lack of parenting, etc.

Where were the parents
Of a bold gun-toting boy
Before Sandy Hook?

1-4-13 – Prompt - Write a poem using these words: Hobby, Tie, Kiss, Porch, Photo

Regret

Sitting on the porch swing
My mind begins to wander,
Your gentle touch and that first kiss
Are thoughts I often ponder.
But there's a photo in my hand
Which ties my thoughts together…
A man on bended knee,
A ring clutched in his hand,
A girl too young to marry
Hoping he'd understand
That she had so much life ahead
And would not yet be tethered.
A stricken look upon your face
As though it were my hobby
To lure a man into my web
And then just leave him sobbing.
And now regret is all I have left
Of bonds so thoughtlessly severed.

1-10-13 –Prompt - Take the phrase "If I Were (Blank)," replace the blank with a word or phrase, make the new phrase the title of your poem, and then write the poem.

Possible titles might be: "If I Were Dreaming," or, "If I Were Upset,"

If I Were Gone

If I were gone
Would you be sad,
Or think it the best news
You ever heard?

If I were gone
Would you replace
My picture on the wall
And soon forget my face?

If I were gone
Would you read again
My pleading, heartfelt poems
Right to their bitter end?

If I were gone…
Don't dwell on how it might be
Perhaps we don't want to know
Perhaps we don't want to see.

If I were gone…
Beware the imagined answer
That can eat away at your heart
Like an undetected cancer.

1-10-13 – Prompt - Write a poem which contains all three of the following elements: Dancing, a pitch-black room, and the smell of lilacs (or flower of your choice)

E-mail Interuptus…

Dancing across the keyboard
Her fingers tapped a happy tune.
The scent of roses by her side
Wafted across the room.
Then suddenly the screen went dark
And her e-mail disappeared
She stomped her feet as the thunder rolled
Then had a thought… and cheered!
Now candles glow in the once dark room
And her frustration has finally dwindled
For she started her email all over again
With an app on her brand new Kindle.

1-18-13 – Prompt - Write a measured poem. I'll let y'all decide what that means. Possibly the poem takes physical measurements or measures one person vs. another. Perhaps it is measured in syllables or stanzas.

Inch by inch by inch
Creeps on the measuring worm
Making his way home

1-18-13 – Prompt - Write a poem about an imaginary city.

Confoundia

There is a place within my mind,
A city resplendent in words.
Towers of knowledge line its streets
And melodious bells can be heard
Ringing the hour and the half.

A library on every corner
With clerks so anxious to please
Happy faces peek from each dormer
Then return to their task with ease,
Separating the good from the chaff.

Search engines move along special streets,
Vehicles designed to go fast
To get straight to the point of your needs
Before your burning desire has passed…
Always working on your behalf.

Awakening was once this city's name
But it changed to Confoundia last year
Since the knowledge for which it was famed
Has faded and will soon disappear.
Its flag is flying half-staff.

Its mayor who once upheld a fine creed
Is now a doddering old fool
Who has let the streets go to weeds
And thinks libraries are outdated tools
Whose hallways now echo his laughs.

So let us mourn for lost knowledge
Which age will bring to us all,
For the empty libraries and college
Which will crumble in Confoundia's fall,
Just one click on life's chronograph.

1-23-13 – Prompt - Write about something others see as ugly but which you see as beautiful.

English Bulldog

Waddling along on legs too short
For the size and weight of his body,
Pushed in nose, drooping jowls
And a smile that tilts quite oddly.
There was a time when even I
Thought the English Bulldog ugly
But the more I look into his sleepy eyes
The more he appears quite snuggly!

1-23-13 – Prompt - Write a fragile poem. That is, write a poem that's either: Delicate in its construction or about a subject that is delicate–literally or figuratively or whatever.

Fragile

From the moment of conception
to our rasping dying breath,
life itself is as fragile
as a long-stemmed ruby rose
whose petals slowly unfurl…
then drop the longer it grows.

Susceptible to sun and drought,
to wind and inclement weather,
the rose stands tall upon her perch
back straight and head held high,
then droops from weary trying
as the long day turns to night.

Just as we are weakened
by the trials of everyday living,
knocked about by circumstance
or beaten down by a broken heart,
we try to stand and face our trials
but droop when our lives fall apart.

From the moment of conception
to our rasping dying breath,
as delicate as the ruby rose
or the meter of a poet's rhyme,
our lives flutter in the breeze
then drift away on the winds of time.

1-30-13 – Prompt - Write a forever poem. The poem could be about things that last forever, take forever, or play on the concept that nothing lasts forever.

Music is ageless
The only thing that changes—
People's opinions

1-30-13 – Prompt - Write about driving with the radio on.

Road Trip

I need my background music
As I sit behind the wheel
And concentrate upon the road
And how the traffic feels.
I can tolerate a good talk show
If it makes me laugh sometimes
And helps the hours pass away
Along that yellow line.

2-5-13 –Prompt - Write about a toy you had as a child.

Ouch!

There were eight little wheels beneath my feet
And a key hung 'round my neck.
A long straight sidewalk
Made its way down our street.
Just outside our gate it waited.

There were eight little wheels beneath my feet
Rolling and turning and bumping the cracks
In that long straight sidewalk
All the way down our street…
Oh the bumps and bruises it created!

2-6-13 – Prompt - Write a poem somehow influenced by an animal. The animal could be the title of the poem, the subject of the poem, a bit part in the poem. Dive into what it means to be animal or non-animal.

Unpredictable

Animal instincts within our genes
Can erupt into wild, rabid terror…
Or nurture the babe within our arms
When motherhood fulfills our dreams.

The trouble is no one can really know
How our instincts will play out over time…
For who can predict what the mind will do
As life shapes the way it will grow?

2-11-13 – Prompt - This being Valentine's week, write a poem about your <u>first</u> love… might not be a person. You figure it out.

That Boy

I can't remember his name now,
That boy with the piercing black eyes,
Who sat across the aisle from me
And never heard my sighs.
I dreamed of him in silence
And played the teenage fool
And never told him how I felt
Way back then in middle school.

2-21-13 – Prompt - Take the phrase "Don't Forget (blank)," replace the blank with a word or phrase, make the new phrase the title of your poem, and then, write your poem.

Don't Forget (…. What?)

You see, that's the problem.
I can't remember what to forget.
One minute's thought is lost the next
Nothing, in my mind, is set.
Thoughts come and go on a whim
Changing from moment to moment
And when it comes to the grocery list
I don't know whether to add or omit!
If I could just hang onto one thought
Long enough to determine its purpose,
I might realize that none of them matter
And each one of them is a surplus!

2-21-13 – Prompt - Write about falling asleep or waking up.

Restless

Falling asleep is easy.
Staying asleep is the problem.
There is no rhyme or reason
To my nightly snoozing agenda.
Tossing and turning side to side
My hip and knee are aching.
Finally I'm sitting up to try
And catch a couple of winks.
Ah, then the light of morning
Peeks brightly through the blinds
And plans for today are forming
In my busy quilter's mind.
Sleep will come later… maybe!

2-25-13 – Prompt - Write about "life in a fishbowl"... literally, or, as they were, being the object of so many stares due to your particular disability or lifestyle. I think you get the idea...

They hide their glances
But one can't miss their rude stares—
Life in a wheelchair

2-27-13 –

Pass It On

Memories are funny things
that twist and turn with time.
I may not remember this or that,
but I know these little oxford shoes
belonged to those babies of mine.
Those tiny little brown and whites –
first shoes for all our boys.
Now more than 50 years ago
when first I slipped them on
those tiny feet – What joy!
Those same shoes warmed the feet
of three wee babes in blue,
and I wanted to pass those memories on
to my first great-grandchild coming soon.
But I learned last night she'll wear a different hue!
Now I need to start thinking pink,
dry my tears, and put the oxfords away,
give up my dream of passing them on,
put them way up on a shelf in a box
with prayers they'll be used….someday!

2-27-13 – Prompt - Write a descending poem. You know the old saying, "Everything that ascends must descend." Okay, maybe it goes a little different than that. Anyway, there's a lot of stuff that descends. Find something and write it!

Composing

Descending notes
On the scale of life
Turning to rise again,
Changing the beat
Of our days and years
Until the melody ends.

3-6-13 – Prompt - Write a knock on wood poem. This might be about a situation that should happen or hopefully will happen... Or I guess it could even involve someone (or something) actually knocking on wood–a table, a door, a window pane, etc.

Knock on Wood

As I gazed out my window this morning
I heard his familiar knock…
Rat-a-tat-tat on the utility pole—
My red-headed woodpecker drummer!
I wonder why his head doesn't ache.
Mine would sure be in shock
If I knocked on wood like that bird does
Even once, not to mention all summer!

3-7-13 – Prompt - With daylight savings time changing this coming weekend, let's use that idea as a prompt. So, write about 1) changing the time, or 2) the changing times

Changing Time

There's only a few more weeks to go
Before it's changing time.
You're getting anxious day by day
But I wonder if you know
Just how fast the days will wind
In these last weeks along the way.
Then soon the cry of a newborn babe
And your heart will skip a beat
At your first sight of your little girl...
This little angel God has saved.
Her grasping hands and tiny feet
Will throw your lives into a whirl
And have you running to and fro
To meet her needs and ignore your own.
Dressing, bathing, watching her sleep,
Around in circles you'll seem to go...
Changing diapers until you're blown
Away by the stress and you weep.
So many changes are on the way
To the life you've come to know
So just stay sweet and loving and kind
For as long as you can today
'cause there's only a few more weeks to go
Before it's changing time.

*****3-13-13 – Prompt -** Write a baby poem.

The poem could be about a human baby, animal baby, or any other type of baby (alien, plant?). Remember: Baby could be an expression used to describe an adult's babyish behavior, or a term of endearment. Heck, I'm sure someone might even try to write a poem about the candy bar that has baby in its name.

See "Changing Time"

*** (Occasionally, when two prompts seem similar or linked, I will use one poem to cover them both as in these two above.)

3-13-13 – Prompt - This week, let's use our senses... any or all of them. Write a poem using all or any of taste, smell, sound, sight, or feeling. Hmmmm...Just occurred to me... These could also be worked into George's prompt to write about a baby.

Baby Powder

No other fragrance
Can bring to mind memories
Of baby-soft skin

Or the look of joy
In baby's first bubbly smile
And in her blue eyes

3-20-13 – Prompt - Write a walking poem. The poem can incorporate any type of walk or form of walking. That includes plays on ideas like the walking dead and dead man walking–or even a Johnny Cash "I Walk the Line" thing-a-ma-do and what-have-you. Keep walking the walk and talking the talk.

Stay at home and exercise
Walk or run or jog
Just don't come complaining to me
When you end up in a fog.

****

Treadclimber -
Pounds will melt away
Tried it once
Doesn't work
Still fat

3-22-13 – Prompt - Write about feeling lonely.

We hug.
We talk.
It's been a long time.
You walk away,
And my heart goes with you.

I am empty,
Defeated…
Life itself
Drawn from my veins,
Alone again.

3-29-13 – Prompt - Write a poem based on the idea of the last of something. Could be a person, place, or thing. The last cookie. The last turn. The last star fighter

Living

Birth – life begins
Childhood – life is learned
Teenage – life is hard, but fun
Adulthood – life is lived or endured
Death – life ends

4-1-13 – Prompt –

A. Write a new arrival poem. The new arrival could be a baby or a person. The new arrival might be a car or other piece of technology. Heck, the new arrival might be an idea or poem.

2013 Toyota Tacoma

Sitting in the yard
Gleaming shiny white…
He finally has his pickup back…
Purchased just last night.

He left behind a trail
Of worthless used car junk
Those "other people's cast-offs"
Kept him in quite a funk.

He had a brand new pickup once
And kept it for three years
Then sold it to our neighbor
Which began our trail of tears.

It's funny how owning a pickup
Can change an old man's mood
For he'll seldom ever drive it,
He'll just stare at it and drool!

B. Prompt - Write a poem about a sofa from your youth.

Plastic… Yuk!

We didn't have much money
When I was just a girl
So Mama tried to protect
Our sofa from the whirl
Of childish dirt and spills.

She covered the sofa and chairs
With plastic furniture throws
And it was indeed protective
For no one sat on it… you know?

It was sticky on bare summer skin
And cool in the winter's chill
But Mama thought it just the thing
And I think it might be there still
If so many years hadn't passed.

So when the plastic covers
Came off each spring for cleaning
That sofa saw more use that day
Than in all the days between!

4-2-13 – Prompt - Write a bright poem or write a dark poem.

Celestial Farewell

As though the hand of God were wiping the wrinkles
from our forehead and the dust of a long day from our eyes,
Night descends in peaceful shades of pink and purple haze
To kiss the day-weary sun adieu as it slips below the horizon.

4-3-13 – Prompt - Write a tentative poem. The poem could be about a tentative date, a tentative person, or a tentative situation. The narrator could be tentative. The subject could be tentative.

Nervous and unsure,
Her fear grows with each glance
At the dentist's chair

4-4-13 –Prompt - Take the phrase "Hold That (Blank)," replace the blank with a word or phrase, make the new phrase the title of your poem, and write the poem. Possible titles include: "Hold That Thought," "Hold That Space," "Hold That Poem," or whatever else holds your attention.

Hold that nail still!
Unintended injuries –
Carpenter's nightmare

4-5-13 – Prompt - Write a plus poem. Plus can mean a lot of things, and even the act of addition could equate to subtraction.

Plus Size

All my life I've been plus size
And not of my own desire.
From a newborn baby's pitiful cries
Through the a lifetime of smoke and fire
I've ended up in my senior years
Still plus size and maybe more,
Still facing my overweight fears,
Still wishing for that firm young core,
Yet knowing I'll never have one
For my joints just won't take the strain.
Just a few stretches and they're all done
While I anticipate tomorrow's pain!
So I guess I'll just settle for plus size,
Although settling is not recommended.
I'll just try to enjoy one day at a time…
If all of you won't be offended!

4-6-13 –Prompt - Write a post poem. Post could be short for post office–or traditional mail. Post could be a wood or metal post. Or post could mean relate to words like postpone, post-punk, or whatever.

Post-It

Take a pad of Post-It notes
And a pen to write things down
And choose a visible spot to post a few.

Write down the chores you think of
Then watch your memory bloom
As you read of all the things you need to do…

But no longer have the energy to start!

4-7-13 – Prompt - Write a sevenling poem. Never heard of a sevenling poem? Well, it's a 7-line poem (chosen because today is the 7th day of the challenge) that features two tercets and a one-liner in the final (third) stanza.

***See previous poem on 4-6-13**

4-8-13 – Prompt - Write an instructional poem. Your instructional poem could list instructions. Or it could capture an instructional moment.

How to Feel Achy 24 Hours A Day

Have a restless, sleepless night.
Don't close your eyes until the dawn.
Awake at eight not feeling right.
Refill the coffee 'til it's gone.
Head out the door to rake up leaves.
Forget to take your morning meds.
As the day grows longer than you believed
Strive to forget the pain in your head.
Don't think about the pain in your hip
Because the pain in your knee is worse.
Then when you just can't make one more trip
You realize you're a victim of stupidity's curse.
You're tired and you're achy from head to toe.
You've overdone it again my friend.
Your night will be restless for that's how it goes
And achy right up 'til the end!

4-9-13 – Prompt - Write one of the following (or both):
* Write a hunter poem. Or * Write a hunted poem

Can't find oven cleaner
Walking the aisles at Walmart
Frustration city!

4-10-13 – Prompt - write a suffering poem. A person or animal in the poem could be suffering.
The poem itself could be suffering.

Faltering Faith

Why does God allow
Pain and suffering to go on?
In His great elaborate plan,
He must have compassion for man!

We pray that His will be done
For He is our Lord and Master.
In His great elaborate plan,
We trust in His compassion for man.

Yet He tests our faith
Each and every long day.
In His great elaborate plan,
Where is His compassion for man?

4-11-13 – Prompt -Take the phrase "In Case of (blank)," replace the blank with a word or phrase, make the new phrase the title of your poem,
and then, write the poem.

In Case of Computer Malfunction

When things are slow working
Or just don't work right
You fear you will lose all your work.
So slip in a flash drive
And save it right now
Before it's gone and you feel like a jerk!

4-12-13 – Prompt - Write a broke poem. The poem could be about a broken record, broken relationship, or someone who is just flat broke (no money).

Experiential Advice

It don't do no good to fuss around
When there ain't no solution to be found
To fix something that's working fine.
If you fix it you may regret it!

Don't fix it if it ain't broke.
Really folks, that ain't no joke!
Just let it be the way it is
And butt-out, get lost, forget it!

4-13-13 – Prompt - Write a comparison poem. The poem could compare one person with another, or it could compare one thing against itself...or it could take a comparable direction.

Decisions!

Starbucks or Keurig—
their recipe or your own
k-cups or teaspoons

decaffeinated
or a big eye opener
milk or heavy cream

coffee, oh coffee
an addiction or desire—
delicioso!

4-14-13 – Prompt - Write a sonnet. For those who are not familiar with the sonnet, it's a 14-line poem that rhymes. [If only it were that easy~!] Some contemporary sonneteers even ditch the rhymes and just write a 14-line poem. Go with whatever feels right.

a b a b
c d c d
e f e f
g g

Without A Thought

I wonder what it's like to write a poem
Without a thought of what it's going to say.
Will your words begin to wander and to roam
And dance about in pure syllabic play…

Or submit to standing quietly in line?
But beware the times they wander out of sight;
They're just waiting for the slightest lapse of mind.
For tomorrow you may forget what made you write

As the mist of age befogs your failing brain,
And the morning hides the visions of the night
While taking pen in hand becomes a strain
For the words play hide and seek from failing sight.

But creating rhyme without a second thought
Is not the way the best of them are wrought!

4-16-13 – Prompt - Write a possible poem or write an impossible poem.

Don't Put Your Blessings on Hold

All things are possible
With faith in the Lord.
Through prayer we may ask
For the needs of our heart.

We must quiet our minds
And gentle our spirits.
Then praise Him and thank Him
From beginning to end.

We may not even know
What to ask for our lives,
But the spirit will help us
Our needs to impart.

So don't think of your prayers
As impossible dreams.
If the good Lord is willing
Great blessings He'll send!

4-17-13 – Prompt - Write an express poem. This might be about an express train or express delivery. It might have something to do with expression painting. However you come at this prompt, be sure to express yourself.

Expressing Myself

I cannot even begin to express
The stupidity of man…
The stupidity and insanity
And crazy, mixed up plans!

I cannot even begin to express
My sadness and regret…
Sadness and regret and shame
For the sickness he begets.

I cannot even begin to express
The prayers within my soul…
Prayers and pleas to God above
To make us once more whole.

To take away the bitterness,
The envy and the greed…
To take away the need to hurt
And plant instead a seed,

A seed of caring, a seed of love,
A seed of reverence and respect,
A seed to grow strong in hope and faith
And all the anger deflect.

No, I cannot even begin to express
My sadness, regret and shame
At being a part of this evil world
And we've only ourselves to blame.

4-18-13 –Prompt - Take the phrase "I Am (blank)," replace the blank with a word or phrase, make the new phrase the title of your poem, and then, write your poem.

Possible titles might include:
"I Am Superman,"
"I Am Wonder Woman,"
"I Am Out of Nickels,"
"I Am Running Low on Patience,"
and so on.

I Am Tired

Of whining men,
Barking dogs,
Crying babies,
And fallen logs…
Rainy days,
Overcast nights,
Loud TVs,
And overbites…
Long commercials,
Failing diets,
Facebook ads,
And undue quiet…
Solicitor calls,
Salesmen's lies,
And bucket lists
Before I die.

Just leave me be
And let me alone.
The light is on
But no one's home!

4-19-13 – Prompt - Write a burn poem. However, burn can represent many things– from getting burned by a bad deal (or a friend) to feeling the burn when working out to physically burning from fires.

Burn – Boston

From the searing pain
Of limbs being ripped
From innocent bodies
To the smoky haze
Obscuring the scene –
Unexpected terror!

Burn – West, TX

From the initial explosion
And flames in the night
To firefighters downed,
Homes and businesses leveled,
Death and destruction –
Unintended terror!

Burn – Brotherly Love

Prayers rise from
The smoke and flames
And hearts across the world
Asking for healing of
Broken bodies and spirits—
Undeniable faith!

4-20-13 – Prompt - Write a beyond poem. The poem could be beyond human comprehension. It could be from the great beyond. It could be from beyond–another city, country, planet, solar system, dimension, etc. Don't be afraid to go above and beyond with it.

(See below)

4-21-13 –Prompt - Write a senryu.

A senryu is like a haiku with less restrictions and different subject matter. It's a 3-line poem with a traditional 5/7/5 syllable (or sound) pattern, and the poem typically deals with the human condition. But that's about all. No cutting words, seasonal words, or focus on nature.

With belief in Christ
Comes faith, hope, love and promise—
Abundant life now.

Eternal life lies
Beyond the Master's promise—
Our heavenly home!

4-22-13 – Prompt - Write a complex poem. Complex is a complex word that can refer to mental state, apartments, difficulty of a situation, and so many other complex situations.

Trying to Figure It Out

The complexities of life
Are hard to understand.
An enigma wrapped in a puzzle
Slipping through our hands.
Even Google cannot map
The lives which God has planned
Nor can it search and find the clues
To explain it all to man.
We can only try to figure it out
And do the best we can
As one day follows another
And our lives, with time, expand.

4-23-13 – Prompt - Write a love poem or an anti-love poem.

See day 24

4-24-13 – Prompt - Write an auto poem. Auto could mean automobile, automatic, automaton,
or any number of possibilities

Great-grandbaby soon.
It will be love at first sight—
It's automatic!

Sweet Baby Girl

You have felt our touch
And heard our voice
And already know the sound of joy
And the touch of love.

You are…

A Seed of hope
Planted with love
And nourished with faith
Sent to provide years
Of blessings!

4-25-13 –Prompt - Take the phrase "Everyone (blank)," replace the blank with a word or phrase,
make the new phrase the title of your poem, and then, write... Possible titles could include: * "Everyone Thinks I'm Crazy," * "Everyone Knows the World Is Round," * "Everyone Needs to Leave Me Alone," or whatever it is that everyone is doing (or not doing).

Everyone's Doing It!

Everyone's doing it!
Haven't you heard?
It's a 30 day tribute
To the poetic word.
Haiku or sonnet
Limerick, cinquain,
Couplet or narrative,
One poem each day.
Write to a prompt
Or make up your own.
The month of April
Is a poetry zone!

4-26-13 – Prompt - Write a casting poem. Casting can take on several meanings, including: casting a spell, casting a line (such as in fishing), casting the actors in a play,
and I suppose even the act of creating a cast.

Fly Casting

I've seen them in pictures and on TV
Whirling their lines overhead.
Fly casting is a fascinating art
Performed by the dedicated fisherman
Who by his hobby is led
To the wild and rushing stream
And the thrill of casting line after line
Of monofilament thread
To get a hook into a fish, then turn
…and set it free!

4-27-13 –Prompt - Write a mechanical poem. Either you're mechanically-inclined, or you're like me and hit things to make them work after they break (which, by the way, rarely works).

"I Love You"

Sometimes it seems mechanical
Called forth by rote, meaningless…
Said only to please the opposite sex
When nothing else will achieve your goal.
        And yet...
Sometimes it seems quite magical
Called forth right from the heart…
Carried on the wings of angels
And dropped gently into your soul.

4-28-13 – Prompt - Write a shadorma.

For those new to the shadorma, it's a fun little 6-line poem that follows this syllable count:
3/5/3/3/7/5.

Seeds of hope
Planted with love and
Nourished with
Faith and joy
Will provide years of blessings
To steadfast parents.

4-29-13 –Prompt - Take a line from one of your poems (preferably one of your April poems), make it the title of your poem today, and then, write...

Among the Rumpled Covers Where You've Lain.

Tossing and turning on long sleepless nights…
Faint visions of yesterday just out of sight.
Thinking of what tomorrow may bring,
Then remembering well betrayal's first sting
And trying to hide the heartbreaking pain
Among the rumpled covers where you've lain.

Holding your pillow to take in your scent.
It lingers there still… a lover's lament.
How many nights of this tossing and turning?
How long the hours of my hopeless yearning
While knowing that only your memory remains
Among the rumpled covers where you've lain?

4-30-13 – Prompt - Pick one (or both):
* Write a finished poem.
* Write a never finished poem.

The "Quick and Easy" Race Quilt

(What a neat idea!
Race to see who finishes first…)

Take 40 fabric strips
Two and one half inches wide
Cut each 42 inches long.

Start with one and join ends with two
Join two to three, etcetera.
Easy as singing a song!

When all the strips are joined
End to end in a line
Pick up number one and forty

And start sewing down the long side.
You sew and sew and sew along
Now this strip is no shorty!

You sew and sew and sew along
And think it will never end
But when you finally reach your goal,
Cut it off even and start again!!

Take one end up to the other
And start sewing down the long side
Do this over and over my friend!

One day soon you will find
Its width and length are right
And your quilt top is ready for trimming.

Then add a border if you wish
And look around the room
To see if you're the one who's winning!

(The next one will be much quicker
For now you've already rehearsed!)

5-8-13 – Prompt - This week people-watch, eavesdrop, and write about your observations or imaginings.

(See 11-6-13)

5-10-13 – Prompt - Write a chapter poem.

This could be the first chapter of a book…or last chapter. It could be the chapter of an organization. Or a chapter of your life.

Final Chapter

If this life of mine was written
As a long and boring book,
Would there be someone to read it
Or to even take a look?

It began in Florida sunshine
On a warm May afternoon
And drifted through a sea of years
Ebbing now too soon.

A final chapter looms ahead
Its days as yet unwritten
Will I make it to my goal,
Or from Heaven be forbidden?

Only God can read the future
And on Him I must depend
To turn the pages and write the lines
'til the final chapter ends.

5-16-13 – Prompt - Write an "on the run" (or "on the loose") poem. Could be a person on the run, or an animal, or even an idea.

I Remember Fun

On the run.
Squeezed in between the job
And the kids
And the housework unending.
I look back on yesterday
Along the way
As all dreams gather in the night
…sleep is near
And a long day is ending.
And I think of here and now
And I vow
To find more time as I run
For some fun
As the days of my life go wending.

5-16-13 – Prompt - Write about city lights at night… might be about their brightness, or their lack of light… could be about the feelings they bring out in you… or as your muse moves you.

City Lights

I've learned that I am somehow drawn
To those city lights at night.
They pull me close and whisper
Of mystery and excitement
In the glow of flashing neon
And darkened alleyways.
It probably has to do with
Thrilling movie madness
The plots and plans and chases
Across the silver screen
Which bring to life another world
That we may never know
In our ordinary lives
between the dusk and dawn.

5-23-13 – Prompt - Write a late poem. Write a poem in which someone or something is late.

Oh God of All...

Spring was a little late this year
And it comes and goes at will...
Sun one day and rain the next,
Snow and hail to follow.
And into the mix a tornado looms
Oh God of all, I'm vexed!
Granted, we are sinners all
Rebellious and unrepentant
And deserving of your ire;
But take it out on the worst of us
And not the innocent children
Lost in blasting wind and fire!

May is late: first weeks wet, windy, cold
Now basking in sunshine.

5-23-13 – Prompt - Write about walking with your eyes closed

Step Lightly

Seems like every day we are together
I'm walking with my eyes closed,
Walking on egg shells,
Never knowing where to step
To avoid the pain of your sharp words
Falling about my feet.

You misunderstand what I try to say,
Twist my words to your own meaning.
I dare not reach out
Or open my eyes to see the truth
But go on walking blindly
Enduring the pain of your words.

5-30-13 – Prompt - Write an unplugged poem.

The plug could be attached to computers, but maybe it's a metaphor for relationships that need the plug pulled. Or a phase of your life. Or a way of thinking. Or a toaster. Just a toaster.

Oh No!

My computer won't come on today
I fear its end is near
I guess I'll take it to the shop
So they can ease my fears.
Oh no, I see the problem!
I think I need a hug...
It doesn't need repair at all;
The danged thing's just unplugged!

5-30-13 – Prompt - Write about someone you admire.

Jesus, Son of God
Forgiveness and grace I seek
Hear my humble prayer

6-6-13 – Prompt - Write a child's play poem. All of us were at one point children. Some of us may be lucky enough to still be children. Certainly, we all know people who act childish.

Mother Goose Adventures

The itsy bitsy spider went up the water spout
And Alice ran into a hole as the rabbit began to shout.
Old Jack Sprat could eat no fat; his wife could eat no lean.
And the three little pigs found out the wolf was really,
 really mean.
Four and twenty blackbirds make a pretty good pie
But all the king's horses and all the king's men
 let Humpty Dumpty die.
As all around the mulberry bush the ants go marching
 one by one,
A cat came fiddling out of a barn just to have some fun.
But then… ding dong bell, pussy's in the well
And five little ducks and five little pigs
 saw just how she fell.
Hark, hark, the dogs do bark in front of the house
 that Jack built
So hush little baby, don't you cry, I love little pussy still.
See... knick, knack, paddy whack I gave the dog a bone
And he got three little Indians to bring the pussy home!

6-6-13 – Prompt - Write a poem from the perspective of your local weatherman.

Weather or Not...

Our programs may try to predict
The path of the upcoming storm
But only God can decide
Its path or its size or its form.
Only God in his infinite plan
Brings the rain or the hail or the wind
And only by his own design
The storm crashes or suddenly ends.
So today as we watch and we wait
Take heed of the warnings you hear
But pray as you go on your way
That God's grace is hovering near!

6-16-13 – Prompt - Take the phrase "Entertain (blank)," replace the blank with a word or phrase, make the new phrase the title of your poem, and then, write your poem. Possible titles include "Entertain the Thought," "Entertain the World," "Entertain Guests,"

Entertain Me!

Make me laugh or make me cry
But don't turn me off or make me sigh
From the stupidity of so much on TV!

Bring me to tears with a poignant story
Or tears of laughter while watching cartoons
But your "reality" is too hard to conceive!

Show me Fred Astaire and Ginger
Or Max and any of his partners
But don't dance around with PSY!

The object here is entertainment...
To captivate, endear, and amaze.
Not make me keep wondering "Why?"

6-18-13 – Prompt - Write a poem in the form of a prayer.

Dear God of all my days
Please hear me as I pray.
As the old year wanes and the new begins
I pray your blessings will now defend
Us from the evil in this world,
The slings and arrows Satan hurls,
And dreams that crash around our feet,
Please help us make our lives replete
With friendships strong and true
All guided by our trust in You.
Please heal our broken spirits Lord
That we might pray in one accord
For good health and hope and peace
For faith renewed and pain to cease.
Please give us the courage to face each day
And rely on You in every way.
Instill in us Your holy flame.
These things we ask in Jesus' name.
Amen

6-19-13 – Prompt - Write a poem using each of the following words somewhere within the poem: cricket, wine, gift, shape

Quiet Time

As evening draws nigh
I sit on my porch and toast
The golden sunset,
A precious gift of God.
Crickets begin their serenade
As the effervescence of
The sparkling wine
Invades my senses
And shapes the course
Of the night to come

7-3-13 –Prompt - For this week's prompt, write an informative poem. This poem could give directions, share news from the outside world, or in some other way inform the reader.

For Your Information:
It rained today... again.

7-10-13 – Prompt - For this week, write a summer poem. Summer can be a good thing – a relaxing time at the beach or on a deck reading a book, for instance. However, summer can also be a time when temperatures rise and tempers flare.

Rain on the window
Days and days of pouring rain –
The grass needs mowing

7-10-13 – Prompt - Listen to a piece of music and write about the images that it brings into your mind.

(Song by Joey and Rory)

When I'm Gone

There will be a day
When I'll be gone...
A time to remember
And reflect...
To think again of
Yesterday...
Of life, love, and loss.

The time will come
To shed a tear
But wipe your eyes
Instead and smile.
I'll be homeward bound.
My work all done.
My soul finally free.

But I'll always be there
When you need me.
I haven't gone so far.
Just listen for my
Voice in the wind
Or feel me in the
Touch of the breeze.

7-15-13 – Prompt - Write a new version of an old fairy tale.

Jack Sprat

Have you ever asked yourself
How Jack Sprat got so lean?
Well ol' Jack joined Weight Watchers you see...
His wife tried too but failed.
Her aversion to lean was too soon seen
In extra pounds on her scales!
Jack weighed in every week.
His wife threw her scales in the trash.
She then signed up for reality TV
And forthwith raked in the cash!
"Why should I bother to diet?" she asked.
And the audience heartily agreed.
"It's so much easier to just indulge
And let the world watch me feed!"

7-17-13 –Prompt - Write an old poem. Now, I don't mean take an already existing poem and pass it off as your own. However, I suppose you could re-write an old poem in a modern style or parody an older poem. Or the poem could be about an older individual, or an older way of thinking,

I May Be Old Fashioned

I may be old fashioned
But I believe in respect
In a world where there is none.

I may be old fashioned
But I believe in Santa Claus
Why miss out on all the fun?

I may be old fashioned
But I believe in love and marriage
And children born in wedlock.

I may be old fashioned
But I believe my ship will come in...
And I'll forget just where it docked!

7-26-13 - Write a charged poem. Maybe it has an electrical charge or a charge to a credit card. Or maybe there's a charge from a bull or a battle charge.

Just say "charge it!"
Pull out the plastic and buy
Your way into debt!

7-30-13 –Prompt - Write about being in prison... If you've never been incarcerated, perhaps you could write about the feeling of being imprisoned, through life circumstances, or whatever.

One Glimmer of Hope

If we make our lives a prison,
We've only ourselves to blame.
We become what we believe;
Bereft, our fears unnamed.
But if we can only find
One glimmer of hope within,
Grab hold and don't let go –
With one glimmer we can win!
God promises never to leave us
And He is faithful to His word.
If we lift our voice to heaven
Our prayers will soon be heard.
He'll send his merciful angels
To unlock the door to our cell
Then He'll walk out beside us
And with us He will dwell.
For if we can only find
One glimmer of hope within
God will turn it into a beacon
Pointing the way to Him.

7-31-13 – Prompt - Write a mistake poem. I guess the poem itself could be a mistake, if you want to go that route, but it could also be a case of mistaken identity, a clerical error, or some other mishap. The narrator of the poem could be sorry for making the mistake or upset that someone else made one.

My Mistake

My mistake is not in wanting to lose weight.
My mistake is in trying to do it
When a "sweet" loving husband's your fate.

"We always had dessert every day
When I was a child growing up...
Pies and cakes made every which way."

But that was then when he worked it off
In the fields and farms of his youth,
Not now when at exercise we scoff.

When we go to get groceries each week
It's not "good for you" veggies
But ice cream and cake that he seeks.

Cookies and donuts and candy "Oh my!"
So there's no way I can diet at all
The temptation is just too great... I sigh.

I always give in and accept my fate
It's too late now to change.
So pass the brownies and don't make me wait"!

8-12-13 –Prompt –

#1 - Write a poem from the point of view of an inanimate object in your home.

Family Photograph

I've been framed and hung,
But you seldom look my way.
Look now, I'm waiting.

#2 - Write a poem about a problem you are currently facing.

Lack of energy,
Extra pounds and achy joints –
Face it! Diet time!

10-20-13

Sticks and Stones…

Sticks and stones may break my bones
But words will never hurt me
Is a saying as old as time itself
But untrue as you will see.
An unkind word can break a heart
And leave it empty, bereft…
Lacking love and friendship
With bitterness all that is left.
A cruel word can cut so deep
That even our soul will bleed.
A thoughtless word can sting
As on our self-esteem it feeds.
So put on the armor of Jesus Christ
To protect your heart and soul
From the sticks and stones of Satan
Being flung at the Master's fold.

11-1-13 – Prompt - Write an appearing poem. This could be a poem about something (or someone) appearing out of nowhere. Or it could be about appearances–appearing one way to some people; appearing another way to others.

Alone?

She appeared to be alone with no companion by her side.
She fiddled with her phone as though trying to decide
If she should call and ask him why she now appeared
to be alone
With teardrops in her eyes and no way of getting home.
Then she felt a gentle touch and saw the young man
at her side
Who took her in his arms and kissed the tears she could
not hide.

11-2-13 – Prompt - Write a “news of the day” poem. The poem should use some sort of recent news event as a springboard. It can be a news story from today (this morning), but it doesn’t have to be.

Police Officer Casey Kohlmeier and his canine, Draco, were killed when their patrol car was struck by a drunk driver on I-55, near mile 201, at approximately 9:30 pm. Their patrol car was in a median turnaround when another vehicle left the northbound lanes and struck them during a period of heavy rain. Officer Kohlmeier and K9 Draco both suffered fatal injuries in the collision. The driver of the other vehicle survived and was subsequently charged with aggravated DUI. Officer Kohlmeier was a U.S. Air Force veteran and had served with the Pontiac Police Department for six years. He was assigned to the Livingston County Proactive Unit. He is survived by his parents

DUI

Four paws that never feared danger,
And a partner who taught him to serve…
Two lives were taken that evening
By rain and a drunken lane-changer.

Parents and co-workers grieve for the team.
Where is the justice for Casey and Draco,
This crime fighting Pontiac duo?
What’s left of their plans and their dreams?

While the rain pelted down all around,
In a flash their patrol car was hit.
In an instant their futures were stolen
And two angels arose heaven bound.

Now badges are all sheathed in black
On the Livingston County force
And a mother and father don’t understand
Why their son is not coming back.

11-3-13 – Prompt - Write a "the last time I was here" poem. Imagine you're returning to a spot (physical, emotional, psychological, etc.): Is it a good thing? Bad thing? What did you leave behind (if anything)? What's there to welcome you back (again, if anything)?

1642 Silver Star Road

It looked so familiar, yet different
As we stopped by the house of my youth.
Its jalousie windows were boarded
Yet it still had the feeling of home.
The orange trees were long since uprooted,
The hydrangeas choked out by weeds,
But walking the ground of my childhood
Made me wonder why I had roamed.
There was where the chicken pen stood
And over there strawberries had bloomed
The fruit picked and sold by my stepfather
As around the neighborhood it was shown.
The old wringer washer had disappeared,
But there was the back porch where it sat.
Mama pinned the clothes on an outside line
For there was no fancy dryer in our home.
My old dog King used to live under there,
Beneath our house supported by blocks.
He wasn't the first pet to die there
And be buried beneath the black loam.
But too many years have come and gone
Too much time has passed in between.
Now I can feel at peace with my past
And bury the fears I had known.

11-4-13 – Prompt - Take the phrase "(blank) Sheet," replace the blank with a word or phrase, make the new phrase the title of your poem, and then write the poem. Possible titles might include: "Rap Sheet," "Blank Sheet," "How to Fold a Sheet," "I Look Like a Ghost beneath This Holey Sheet,"

Short Sheet

Cold feet?
No heat?
Short sheet!

11-5-13 – Prompt –

#1. Write a concealed poem. Could be about a concealed weapon, concealing emotions, concealing intentions, etc. Cover it up and write about it.

#2. Write an unconcealed poem. Okay, take everything from the first prompt and uncover it. Reveal everything that's hidden.

(Untitled)

Another windy November day,
Leaves playing tag on the breeze.
Dragonfly hovers, watching,
Futuristic drone, spying…
Intentions hidden,
Unknown.

11-6-13 –Prompt - Write a poem from the perspective of a person who either works at and/or visits a place you like to visit (someone other than yourself). For instance: a fry chef at the Krusty Krab, a bouncer at a nightclub, a waitress at a restaurant, etc.

Take This Job and Shove It! (Walmart cashier)

Why can't these people count?
It says "20 Items or Less!"
Yet 30 or 40 will come across…
I'm frustrated, I must confess.
I stand on my feet for hours
I'm tired and my back really aches.
I wait and wait for my relief.
It's way past time for my break!
I can't get the schedule I want.
My kids miss me at home.
I can't afford a sitter;
But, I can't leave them alone.
Life is hard for a single mom.
New problems arise each day,
And I would not be doing this work
If there was any other way!
So take this job and shove it
Up where the sun don't shine;
And if you don't you'll just hear me
Continue my work-a-day whine!

11-7-13 – Prompt - Write a hardship poem. The hardship could be moving forward after a tragic loss, having to work through a difficult problem, or even just showing up to work. It can be serious, funny, or complicate

Typhoon Haiyan

Unbearable fear
Inescapable terror
Death on the wind and the waves
Panic in the air
Screams in the night
Memories of those who were saved

11-8-13 –Prompt - Write an inanimate object poem. Obviously, you could write an objective poem about an inanimate object, or you can write from the perspective of the inanimate object. If you can think of a third option, have at it.

Pulled and stretched
Rolled out upon the surface –
Measuring tape

11-9-13 – Prompt - Take the phrase “The Other (blank),” replace the blank with a word or phrase, make the new phrase the title of your poem, and then, write your poem. Some possible titles may include: “The Other Side of the Story,” “The Other Brother,” “The Other Hand,” or whatever else you concoct.

The Other Day

The other day I wandered
Down a path of no return.
And wondered why I found
No other way to get back home.
On the other side of the road
The chicken lost his way
Looking for greener grass
On the tempting other side.
On the other hand I learned
To check my moral compass
To be sure my path is straight
And no other lure misguides me.

11-10-13 – Prompt - Write a poem incorporating something sweet. Maybe a cake or pie. Possibly a candy bar or pixie stick (you know, that paper straw with delicious sugar inside–mmm). Or move it sweetly in another direction.

Dump Cake

Preheat oven to 350 degrees
Take one 20 oz. can or crushed pineapple and **dump it**
Into a 9 x 13 inch dish if you please.

Take one 21 oz. can of cherry pie filling and **dump it**
Atop the pineapple in big globs of red.

Take one box of yellow cake mix and **dump it**
Evenly over the fruit now in the dish bed.

Cut two sticks of butter into slices and **dump it**
Randomly over the cake mix.

Take ¼ cup nuts of your choice and **dump it**
All over the cake you have fixed.

Bake one hour at 350 degrees and then **dump it**
By spoonsful onto your plate.

Sweeten it up with some whipped cream and **dump it**
Into your mouth and you'll think it's just great!

11-11-13 – Prompt - We're going to write ekphrastic poetry–or poetry based off another piece of art.

[For ekphrastic poetry, poets use art as a prompt for their poetry. Often, the poems are a response or an elaboration of the original art - which makes this prompt a bit different/difficult.]

In the past, I've provided paintings, but today, I'm picking photographs (for something a little different).

African skyscrapers
Sentinels of the plains
Giraffes on patrol

11-12-13 – Prompt -

#1. Write a poem about your happiest moment. Well, doesn't have to be yours actually. Just a moment that is someone's happiest. - or -

#2. Write a poem about your saddest moment. Conversely, take happy, flip it, and make it the saddest moment.

My Happiest Moment

I am not a wildly "happy" person.
I walk around with a scowl on my face.
I've known people who laughed all the time.
Their laughter flowing easily and unbidden.
I laugh sometimes, but not often…
Contemplative, that's what I am.
To choose my happiest moment
Would be like asking a diner to choose
His favorite dish in a mediocre buffet.
I wasted many long years waiting
For someone else to make me "happy."
Then I finally learned that I am the only one
Responsible for my own happiness
And I set out to find it on my own.
But happiness is still as illusive
As the Great Pumpkin on Halloween.
One day perhaps I will come across
That "happiest moment"
And write an ode to happiness….
One day… maybe.

11-13-13 – Prompt - Write a self-help poem. It can be written in the style of a self-help article or book. Or you can take it in a more subtle self-help direction.

Helping Myself

I've helped myself to too many cookies
And brownies and cake in a cup...
I get on the scales and I want to scream
As the numbers climb up and up.
At my age I ought to be able to enjoy
All the goodies that youth kept at bay.
There's no need now to impress anyone
I'm not lookin' for love… not today!
So why can't those calories be slipperier
And not cling so tightly to my hips?
I guess I'll just have to give up
All those Doritos and yummy chip dip!
If I'm to help myself become slimmer
I'll need a new frame of mind.
So keep telling me just how good I look…
Lie a little, just try to be kind!

11-16-13 - , Prompt - Write a half-way poem. The poem might deal with a half-way point in time. Or perhaps, a place in the dead center of here and there. Even a compromise on terms in a negotiation can work.

Stuck in the middle
Halfway between birth and death –
Mid-life crisis!

11-17-13 – Prompt - Write an element poem. Maybe an element from the periodic table (hydrogen, oxygen, etc.). Maybe an element of surprise?!? Or a missing element, which could refer to a person, tool, or poem. Run wild with it.

Elemental

"It's elemental Mr. Watson,"
Sherlock Holmes used to say
The basic facts of any case
May lead you all the way.
So look closely at the details
Try to see what's hidden from view.
Look into the mind of the criminal
And let the scene talk to you.

(Continued in the next prompt)

11-18-13 – Prompt - Write a "forget what I said earlier" poem. This poem could be a response to a poem you wrote earlier in the challenge (or just earlier in general). Or it could cover one of those moments–I have them all the time–when you say something that ends up proving wrong or that you wish you'd taken back

Now forget what I said earlier
And think outside the box.
Sometimes the basics may lead you astray
And you find your way has been blocked.
There's a secret message within each clue
A code that you must break,
And whatever you do to solve the case,
You do for the victim's sake.

11-19-13 – Prompt - Write a love poem. Romantic or more general types of love. Or… Write an anti-love poem. Some folks just don't like love poems of any type, so have at it

Tova

Smiles and giggles
And sparkling eyes
Bubbles and burps
And looking surprised
Eyes open wide
And chubby cheeks
A word of warning…
Watch out! She leaks!
Great-granddaughter
We love you dear
And pray God holds you
Ever near.

11-20-13 – Prompt - Take the phrase “Always (blank),” replace the blank with a new word or phrase, make the new phrase the title of your poem, and then, write your poem. Possible titles include: “Always on My Mind,” "Always Wrong,” “Always Writing Poems That Don’t Sound as Good the Next Day,” etc.

Always Quilting

The thoughts in my head
keep revolving
‘round fabric and
colorful thread.

From thought to creation,
design, cut and sew,
sandwich and quilt...
all here in my head.

I never had thought
to sew night and day.
From dream to machine…
It’s not work - it’s play!

11-22-13 – Prompt - Write a poem using at least three of the following six words:

ideogram - symbol that represents an idea or object
remora – an obstruction,
casket,
eclipse,
selfie,
wretch

Use the words in the title of your poem, in the body of your poem, and feel free to play with them (by which, I mean, make them plural, past tense, etc.).

Selfie

I took a selfie the other day
And it made me want to wretch.
This wrinkle-faced, old woman
Eclipsed all other younger,
More beautiful memories
Of the woman
I once knew.

11-24-13 – Prompt - Write a poem that responds to a statement. You can use any statement, quote, etc., that you wish, but I've included a few to make it easier. That said, feel free to find and use a different statement for your poem.

The Statement:

"Everyone has a built-in, Happiness-Now Button,
that can instantly change how they feel.
Go on, push it real good."
--Mike Dooley

The Response:

I don't know what it would take
To find my "Happiness-Now" button
Perhaps if I could lose some weight
And not be such a glutton
Happiness might find me.

I do, however, have a "Rage" button
Which must have neon lights
My husband knows just how to push it
And make me want to fight.
It's quite the sight to see.

I even have an "Off" button
Which makes me withdraw within
It sends me into silent mode
Wishing my troubles would end
And makes me want to flee!

PROMPT RESPONSE

Happiness, rage, or depression,
Complex emotions are these,
As close as the flip of a switch
For those who wish to tease
Or their own immense ego appease.

11-25-13 – Prompt - Take a poem from earlier in the challenge (that you've written) and remix it. You could take a free verse poem and re-work it into a villanelle or shadorma.

You could re-work multiple poems into a new one. You could take a line from one of the poems and write a response poem to it. Or you can take it in an entirely different direction.

A remix of this poem:

The Other Day

The other day I wandered
Down a path of no return.
And wondered why I found
No other way to get back home.
On the other side of the road
The chicken lost his way
Looking for greener grass
On the tempting other side.
On the other hand I learned
To check my moral compass
To be sure my path is straight

… into a Haiku

The other day
I wandered off the path -
misguided by love

11-26-13 –Prompt –

 # 1. Take the phrase "Free (blank),"replace the blank with a word or phrase and make the new phrase the title of your poem, and then, write your poem. Example titles might include: "Free Bird," "Freedom Isn't Free,"

"Free Offer," etc.

Free Hugs

My arms are open wide
Just come and step inside!

#2. Take the phrase "(blank) Free," replace the blank with a word or phrase, make the new phrase the title of your poem and then, write your poem. Example titles might include: "Fat Free," "Stone Free," "How to Be Free," etc.

Born Free

Like the bird which is fed in its nest
By a devotion as old as time
God feeds us with His Word
So loving, so healing, so kind.
As His birds are truly born free
To choose to fly or to fall
We too have freedom of choice
To sin or to answer His call.
So take wing like a chick from its nest
Fly high as you follow His Word
Then join the birds in joyful song
Let freedom's music be heard!

11-27-13 –Prompt - Write a local poem.

By local, I'm thinking of something that happens or has happened in your neck of the woods, but you know, I'm never against poets bending and/or breaking my rules.

Local News

The local news is far from new
When it comes but once a week.
A lot can happen in seven days
Which we should have known right away!
So give me the big city paper
With its daily report of events.
Its timely news keeps us informed
And allows us to plan out our days.

(With compliments to hardisonink.com, our rural *daily* online news team)

11-28-13 – Prompt - Write a bird poem. Pick a bird, any bird, and write a poem about it. Or just write a poem that happens to have a bird somewhere in it.

Motorhomes head out
Snow-birds fleeing winter's cold –
Seeking southern warmth

Geese fly overhead
The true snow-birds from the north –
Seeking southern warmth

*** or ***

Hunger driven
Colorful combatants –
Hummingbirds feed

11-29-13 – Prompt - Write a commercial poem. This prompt makes me think about the commercialism decried in 'Merry Christmas, Charlie Brown," but there are any number of ways to attack a commercial poem.

Sew What?

Yes, this is a blatant commercial,
A plea for my business to grow.
I'm making quilts and purses
And I want you all to know
You can find them online at Sew What?
My store at wix.com.
Go to sew-what-quilts.biz,
Buy something now for your Mom!
Christmas will soon be upon us
Don't wait 'til it's too late to mail!
Help Santa arrive on time!
Order now, get with it, don't fail!
(http://www.sew-what-quilts.biz)

11-30-13 – Prompt - Write a disappearing poem. Simple as that.

Waves of Sadness

The joy of a family reunion
With children from far away
Is eclipsed by their departure
For I wish that they could stay.
Now I watch their flights take wing
And my joy disappears in tears
Replaced by waves of sadness
And a mother's unending fears.
They return to lives of their own,
Unconnected it seems to mine,
As my life fades from day to day
With the shifting sands of time.

12-5-13

Home

We fall in love and get married
And then the children come along
We learn and grow together
And share each other's woes.
And then comes graduation day
Or marriage, or employment
And the kids all move away
Leaving us here so alone.
They come to visit now and then
But it's never quite the same
This place just seems so empty…
This place that we call home.

A church is like a family
Brothers and sisters of one accord
We learn and grow together
And share each other's woes.
And then some start to stray,
Just leave or disappear,
Or join a different church
Leaving us here so alone.
They may come to visit now and then
But it's never quite the same
And the pews just seem so empty…
In this church that we call home.

Dear Lord I miss my family…
My children have moved away,
And the family I found at church
Have all begun to roam.
Our membership is dwindling
Though the sermons are all well said
I don't know how to bring them back
I'm feeling so sad and alone.
Please keep your angels by their side
And protect them day by day
And let them know they're still welcome here
At this place they once called home

12-12-13 – Prompt - Write an antique poem. It could be about or involve physical antiques. Or maybe the poem addresses an antique way of thinking, acting, etc.

Look at me –
If I am not an antique,
I don't know what is!

12-19-13 – Prompt - Write a someday poem. By someday poem, I mean that you should write a poem about someday in the future. However, I'm always more than open to poets taking the prompt in any direction they wish.

Revelation 21:1 – And I saw a new heaven and a new earth: for the first heaven and the first earth were passed away...

Revelation 21:4 – And God shall wipe away all tears from their eyes; and there shall be no more death, neither sorrow, nor crying, neither shall there be any more pain; for the former things are passed away.

Come Lord Jesus!
We await your perfect "someday",
A time when all we know will be refreshed, renewed:
Tears will not flow, death will be defeated;
We will not mourn, or weep,
Or feel the sting of pain.
We have kept the faith!
We have endured for You!
Come Lord Jesus
And take us home
Into that perfect "someday!"

12-25-13 –Prompt - Write a gift poem. Giving gifts, receiving gifts, coveting the gifts of others, admiring gifts, planning gifts, and so on. Consider this prompt a gift from me.

Gone!

That Christmas gift you cannot stand?
Don't worry Dear. We have a plan.
If it just doesn't make you feel uplifted,
Wait a few months and then re-gift it!

12-31-13 –Prompt - Write a New Year's poem.

The ball drops
And spirits rise
To meet the New Year
Shivering
In anticipation

1-1-14 –Prompt - Write a weird poem. Maybe it's a twist ending or a person on another planet (or in another time). Maybe it's a land in which weird people are those that look just like us. Or whatever floats your boat.

Isn't it weird
How you feel let down
The day after the big celebration?
After all the fuss and falderal,
And the mess has been cleared away,
Where is the hope of elation?
Today is just another day,
The first page of another year…
Awaiting your imagination!

With this first poem of 2014 I leave you to wonder just where my imagination will take me in the months to come.

God bless you and may this year be all you hoped for and even better than you ever dreamed!

Ruth Y. Nott

PROMPT RESPONSE

Printed in Great Britain
by Amazon